5-MINUTE EVENING INTENTION JOURNAL

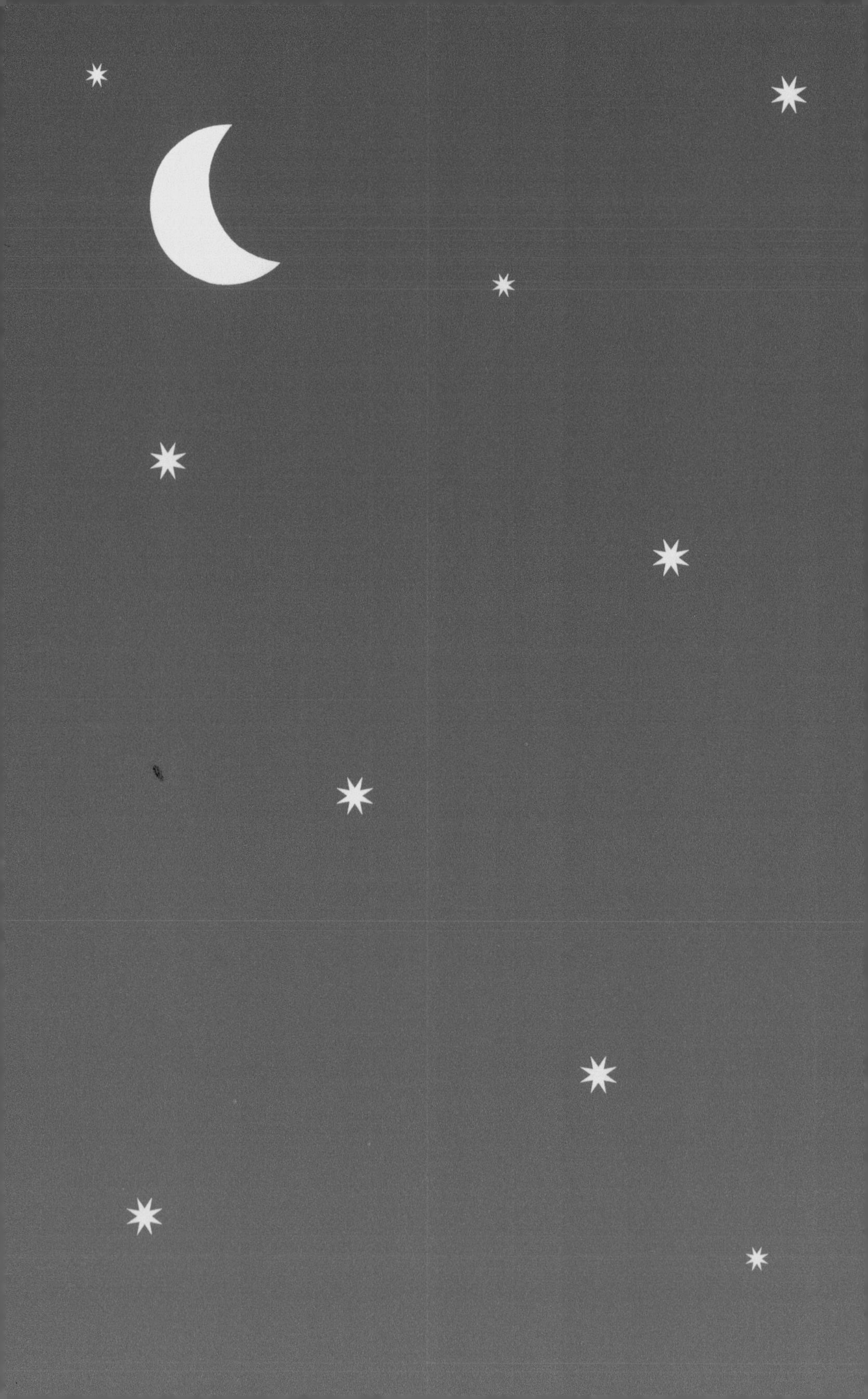

5-minute evening intention journal

**INSPIRING PROMPTS
TO SET INTENTIONS
AND END YOUR
DAY WITH GRATITUDE**

TANYA J. PETERSON, MS, NCC

ROCKRIDGE
PRESS

For general information on our other products and services or to obtain technical support, please contact our Customer Care Department within the United States at (866) 744-2665, or outside the United States at (510) 253-0500.

Rockridge Press publishes its books in a variety of electronic and print formats. Some content that appears in print may not be available in electronic books, and vice versa.

Interior and Cover Designer: Diana Haas
Art Producer: Alyssa Williams
Editor: Adrian Potts
Production Editor: Ellina Litmanovich
Production Manager: Riley Hoffman

Paperback ISBN: 978-1-63878-092-2
eBook ISBN: 978-1-63807-772-5
R0

THIS JOURNAL IS DEDICATED
TO YOU. CONGRATULATIONS FOR
TAKING CHARGE OF YOURSELF,
YOUR LIFE, AND HOW YOU LIVE.
YOU'VE GOT THIS!

Contents

INTRODUCTION x

GRATEFUL FOR MEANINGFUL WORK 1
WORK–LIFE BALANCE 1
MASTERING SKILLS 13
REWARDS FOR EFFORT 25

GRATEFUL FOR SOCIAL WELLBEING 37
AUTHENTIC SELF 37
MEANINGFUL RELATIONSHIPS 49
SOCIAL SUPPORT NETWORK 61

GRATEFUL FOR FINANCIAL WISDOM 73
NEEDS VERSUS WANTS 73
SPENDING MINDFULLY 85
SAVING FOR FUTURE GOALS 97

GRATEFUL FOR MY BODY 109
HEALTH AND MOOD 109
BODY IMAGE 121
GETTING STRONGER 133

GRATEFUL FOR COMMUNITY 145
VALUING DIVERSITY 145
WORKING TOWARD COMMON GOALS 157
SERVICE TO OTHERS 169

RESOURCES 181
REFERENCES 183

This Journal Belongs to

_____

Introduction

WELCOME TO THIS JOURNAL and your journey toward greater purpose
and peace. As you'll discover, spending just five minutes at night with
this cozy and uplifting journal will help you process the day, redirect
your mind from any worries, and transition gently into a restful sleep.

By using these pages, you are gifting yourself with the opportunity
to reflect on the happenings of the day, check in with your thoughts and
feelings, and accept where you are at. You can focus on what has gone
well, express gratitude for the good in your life, and call to mind what is
important to you for the day ahead.

I've written *5-Minute Evening Intention Journal* to help you live your
life with intention. This is the opposite of living on autopilot, when you
are driven and controlled by forces outside of you. To live with intention is to live life on purpose and on your terms. Living like this, guided
by your personal values and responding rather than reacting to life,
requires planning. This journal can help you do that as you connect
with and reflect on what is most meaningful to you.

Having worked as a teacher and certified counselor with people of
all ages, I often suggest journaling as a way for anyone to take charge
of their lives and flourish. People have shared with me how much
journaling has helped them create clarity in their lives. Exploring
both problems and possibilities has helped many individuals shape
an authentically positive perspective so they can live with gratitude,
intention, and joy.

I've come to cherish journaling in my personal life, and it's a part of
my day I look forward to. It's a chance to pause and nurture myself so
I can live my best life. Journaling allows me to create my life as I live
it and make adjustments and improvements while I remain focused
on meaning and gratitude. I used to live with significant anxiety, and
dealing with chronic stress contributed to my serious autoimmune and
digestive disorders. Journaling has been an important practice for me
through these and other challenges, including a traumatic brain injury.

While you get to determine just how frequently you want to write,
a regular journaling practice will help you shape your own direction,

actions, and thoughts. You'll develop a healthier relationship with the emotions that constantly flow into and out of our lives. As you relax into writing, you'll recap your day so you can celebrate your accomplishments, deal positively with challenges, express gratitude for the good, and set your intentions for tomorrow. Your evening journaling practice will help you step out of your mind—your thoughts about life—and into the moments of your life itself. You can live the rich life that you very much deserve.

THE BEST WAY TO END YOUR DAY

Journaling for wellbeing, gratitude, and intention is most effective when done regularly. "Regularly," though, is personal. This is *your* journal for living your life on your terms, so please don't feel pressured to use it every evening. Feeling like you must use it daily can quickly become overwhelming and burdensome. Make your practice joyful and something you look forward to, rather than just one more exhausting task you must accomplish before you can finally go to bed.

You will benefit from the journal even if you can't engage with it every night. I do, however, encourage you to create a routine for your journaling time, whether that's three nights a week, on the weekends, or on other specific days. Research suggests that a regular journaling practice can be transformative.

* In a 2010 positive psychology research project at Arkansas State University, students who practiced mindfulness as well as gratitude and reappraisal journaling (reflecting on challenges to make sense of them) experienced greater acceptance of difficulties, an increase in positive thoughts, and reduced negativity.
* A study published in 2017 in the *Journal of Nursing Education and Practice* revealed that journaling significantly increased compassion satisfaction while decreasing compassion fatigue and burnout among registered nurses. In the study, 66 nurses journaled regularly for six weeks and reported benefits, including the ability to release pressure and stress and feeling more comfortable and better connected with themselves.
* When done regularly, journaling about intentions and gratitude boosts the ability to handle stress and helps people focus on the

positives in their lives that are otherwise overshadowed by problems and negativity, according to a report published in 2019 by the National Institutes of Health.

* A 2011 study in the journal *International Association for Applied Psychology: Health and Well-Being* investigated the effectiveness of nightly journaling on sleep. Journaling every night for one week helped university students decrease worry and stress, resulting in better and longer sleep.

Establishing a comforting nightly journaling routine brings unique benefits. Reflecting on your day before you settle into sleep helps you develop a new, healthy relationship with your day and night. Journaling to let go of difficulties can become a soothing part of your wind-down routine that helps you sleep better. It also sets you up for success the next day as you create your intentions for your life, and writing about things for which you are grateful helps you choose your focus.

Spending just five minutes in the evening to reflect on your thoughts, cultivate gratitude, and set intentions allows you to end your day on a positive note. Imagine drifting off to sleep with a light heart and calm mind and waking up refreshed and ready to embrace a new day!

"You don't know what kind of day you will have, until evening."

—SOPHOCLES

HOW TO RELISH THIS JOURNAL—
AND REFLECT UPON YOUR DAY

You'll discover two types of exercises in this evening journal: Daily Journal Pages and Inspiration Pages. Together they will guide you in reflecting on yourself, your experiences, and your aspirations for who you want to be and how you want to shape your life.

Daily Journal Pages: These make up the majority of the journal, offering a space to reflect on what you were grateful for in the day, note any challenges or accomplishments, track your intentions, and write about anything else that's on your mind. While the journal is divided into different themes, on the Daily Journal Pages you can write about any topic or area of your life that you wish. You can find a preview of what these pages look like on xvi.

Inspiration Pages: These are peppered throughout the book, allowing you to focus a specific theme related to your wellbeing. They all center on gratitude for specific aspects of your life to help you identify the positive that exists among life's challenges. You'll have a chance to contemplate meaningful work, social wellbeing, financial wisdom, your body, and community. Your exploration will invite you to progress toward goals, growth, and a sense of fulfillment. You can find a preview of how these pages are designed on page xvii.

Be confident knowing that this journal is informed and inspired by widely accepted principles of our core human needs. According to the late and well-respected psychologist Abraham Maslow, we all are motivated by fundamental requirements. To thrive, we must fulfill five different levels of needs that build on each other in a hierarchy.

1. First we must meet our basic physiological needs, such as nourishment, rest, and health.

2. Next comes safety, including shelter, resources, and security.

3. Once these are met, we are driven to meet psychological needs, which encompass belonging, connection, intimacy, and love.

4. This leads to esteem, which consists of feeling competent and accomplished.

5. Finally, we progress to pursue self-actualization, a sense of being guided from within rather than controlled by others or our circumstances, and working toward growth and positive choices.

Most, if not all, of the challenges we face in our lives fall into the realm of this hierarchy of human needs. I've structured this journal to blend with these needs so they fit intimately with what you need, not just to survive in your life, but to thrive. The personal concepts you reflect on—things that challenge you and those that make you feel grateful—will help you identify which of your needs could benefit from your nurturing attention. This will help you set meaningful intentions to guide you toward a life of purpose.

Turn the page for peek at the prompts you'll discover in the journal.

DAILY JOURNAL OVERVIEW

ACCOMPLISHMENT: **TODAY, I ACHIEVED** . . .

What things, no matter how big or small, did you achieve today? How did your intentions support your actions and accomplishments?

CHALLENGE: **I WAS FACED WITH** . . .

What challenge surfaced today, and how did you respond to work toward solving it? Capture your reflections here without judging them or yourself.

GRATITUDE: **I'M GRATEFUL FOR** . . .

What went well today? What positive experiences did you enjoy? Capture anything, big or small, for which you feel grateful today.

INTENTION: **TOMORROW I WILL** . . .

What is your vision for yourself and your day tomorrow? How will this shape your thoughts, attitude, motivation, and actions for the day ahead?

SPACE: **ON MY MIND / IN MY HEART / ON MY SHOULDERS / LIGHTING MY WAY** . . .

What inspires you? What is most important to you? What is nearest and dearest to your heart?

INSPIRATION PAGE OVERVIEW

THEME

Each page features a daily theme connected to the hierarchy of human needs to guide your thoughts and intentions in fresh directions.

TITLE

This is the focal point for the day's theme.

RELATED QUOTE

You'll find inspiring quotes related to the theme to energize, motivate, and help you think in new, positive ways.

REFLECTION

This is an expanded consideration of today's theme to help you apply it to your own life.

SELF-INQUIRY INVITATIONS

You can respond to the prompts that help you explore and enhance your own thoughts, feelings, and experiences as you expand your sense of well-being, gratitude, and purpose.

"We need to do a better job
of putting ourselves higher on
our own 'to do' list."

—MICHELLE OBAMA

GRATEFUL FOR MEANINGFUL WORK

WORK–LIFE BALANCE

✳ ✳ ✳

REFLECTION

Whether your work is paid or unpaid, having long to-do lists that require time and effort can be overwhelming. Often it's not the work itself that is damaging to our wellbeing but instead is a lack of balance. Research has shown that creating boundaries between what you must do and what you want to do is a buffer that protects you from stress and the host of negative mental and physical health effects that come with it.

SELF-INQUIRY INVITATIONS

Boost your awareness. As you think of your work, what positive and negative emotions arise? Name them as specifically as you can.

* Our feelings can guide us in creating balance. What changes could you make in how you move toward your work and non-work goals?
* Reflect on the things that are most important to you in your work and in your non-work time, and list them here.
* What are you willing to sacrifice to manifest those things that are important to you in both realms of your life? For how long would you want to make these sacrifices?

✱ ✱ ✱

ACCOMPLISHMENT: **TODAY, I ACHIEVED . . .**

....

....

CHALLENGE: **I WAS FACED WITH . . .**

....

....

GRATITUDE: **I'M GRATEFUL FOR . . .**

....

....

INTENTION: **TOMORROW I WILL . . .**

....

....

SPACE: **ON MY MIND / IN MY HEART /
ON MY SHOULDERS / LIGHTING MY WAY . . .**

....

....

....

....

✳ ✳ ✳

ACCOMPLISHMENT: **TODAY, I ACHIEVED . . .**

....

....

CHALLENGE: **I WAS FACED WITH . . .**

....

....

GRATITUDE: **I'M GRATEFUL FOR . . .**

....

....

INTENTION: **TOMORROW I WILL . . .**

....

....

SPACE: **ON MY MIND / IN MY HEART /
ON MY SHOULDERS / LIGHTING MY WAY . . .**

....

....

....

....

ACCOMPLISHMENT: **TODAY, I ACHIEVED . . .**

CHALLENGE: **I WAS FACED WITH . . .**

GRATITUDE: **I'M GRATEFUL FOR . . .**

INTENTION: **TOMORROW I WILL . . .**

SPACE: **ON MY MIND / IN MY HEART /
ON MY SHOULDERS / LIGHTING MY WAY . . .**

✳ ✳ ✳

ACCOMPLISHMENT: **TODAY, I ACHIEVED . . .**

CHALLENGE: **I WAS FACED WITH . . .**

GRATITUDE: **I'M GRATEFUL FOR . . .**

INTENTION: **TOMORROW I WILL . . .**

SPACE: **ON MY MIND / IN MY HEART /
ON MY SHOULDERS / LIGHTING MY WAY . . .**

ACCOMPLISHMENT: **TODAY, I ACHIEVED . . .**

_____

_____

CHALLENGE: **I WAS FACED WITH . . .**

_____

_____

GRATITUDE: **I'M GRATEFUL FOR . . .**

_____

_____

INTENTION: **TOMORROW I WILL . . .**

_____

_____

SPACE: **ON MY MIND / IN MY HEART /
ON MY SHOULDERS / LIGHTING MY WAY . . .**

_____

_____

_____

_____

_____

✳ ✳ ✳

ACCOMPLISHMENT: **TODAY, I ACHIEVED . . .**

CHALLENGE: **I WAS FACED WITH . . .**

GRATITUDE: **I'M GRATEFUL FOR . . .**

INTENTION: **TOMORROW I WILL . . .**

SPACE: **ON MY MIND / IN MY HEART /
ON MY SHOULDERS / LIGHTING MY WAY . . .**

ACCOMPLISHMENT: **TODAY, I ACHIEVED . . .**

CHALLENGE: **I WAS FACED WITH . . .**

GRATITUDE: **I'M GRATEFUL FOR . . .**

INTENTION: **TOMORROW I WILL . . .**

SPACE: **ON MY MIND / IN MY HEART /
ON MY SHOULDERS / LIGHTING MY WAY . . .**

✳ ✳ ✳

ACCOMPLISHMENT: **TODAY, I ACHIEVED . . .**

....

....

CHALLENGE: **I WAS FACED WITH . . .**

....

....

GRATITUDE: **I'M GRATEFUL FOR . . .**

....

....

INTENTION: **TOMORROW I WILL . . .**

....

....

SPACE: **ON MY MIND / IN MY HEART /
ON MY SHOULDERS / LIGHTING MY WAY . . .**

....

....

....

....

"You can't stop the waves, but you can learn to surf."

—JON KABAT-ZINN

GRATEFUL FOR MEANINGFUL WORK

MASTERING SKILLS

REFLECTION

Our work is often most meaningful when we feel like we can bring our best selves to our tasks. Being able to use your unique skills, abilities, talents, and strengths has been shown to contribute to wellbeing and life satisfaction. Learning and mastering new skills can add richness and depth to your daily work, or it can inspire you to take your work in a new direction and pursue something that allows you to use your abilities to feel fulfilled.

SELF-INQUIRY INVITATIONS

* Reflect on your passions—the things that make you feel most alive and energized in your heart, mind, and spirit. What skills allow you to pursue them?
* List some of the skills, abilities, and personal strengths you are most proud of. How do you use these in your work? Are there new ways you can apply them?
* Are there new skills you'd like to develop? How would learning a new skill enhance your work and make it more meaningful?
* What do you need in order to learn this new skill or develop an existing one?

ACCOMPLISHMENT: **TODAY, I ACHIEVED . . .**

....

....

CHALLENGE: **I WAS FACED WITH . . .**

....

....

GRATITUDE: **I'M GRATEFUL FOR . . .**

....

....

INTENTION: **TOMORROW I WILL . . .**

....

....

SPACE: **ON MY MIND / IN MY HEART /
ON MY SHOULDERS / LIGHTING MY WAY . . .**

....

....

....

....

....

✳ ✳ ✳

ACCOMPLISHMENT: **TODAY, I ACHIEVED . . .**

....

....

CHALLENGE: **I WAS FACED WITH . . .**

....

....

GRATITUDE: **I'M GRATEFUL FOR . . .**

....

....

INTENTION: **TOMORROW I WILL . . .**

....

....

SPACE: **ON MY MIND / IN MY HEART /
ON MY SHOULDERS / LIGHTING MY WAY . . .**

....

....

....

....

....

ACCOMPLISHMENT: **TODAY, I ACHIEVED . . .**

....

....

CHALLENGE: **I WAS FACED WITH . . .**

....

....

GRATITUDE: **I'M GRATEFUL FOR . . .**

....

....

INTENTION: **TOMORROW I WILL . . .**

....

....

SPACE: **ON MY MIND / IN MY HEART /
ON MY SHOULDERS / LIGHTING MY WAY . . .**

....

....

....

....

✳ ✳ ✳

ACCOMPLISHMENT: **TODAY, I ACHIEVED . . .**

....

....

CHALLENGE: **I WAS FACED WITH . . .**

....

....

GRATITUDE: **I'M GRATEFUL FOR . . .**

....

....

INTENTION: **TOMORROW I WILL . . .**

....

....

SPACE: **ON MY MIND / IN MY HEART /
ON MY SHOULDERS / LIGHTING MY WAY . . .**

....

....

....

....

....

✳ ✳ ✳

ACCOMPLISHMENT: **TODAY, I ACHIEVED . . .**

....

....

CHALLENGE: **I WAS FACED WITH . . .**

....

....

GRATITUDE: **I'M GRATEFUL FOR . . .**

....

....

INTENTION: **TOMORROW I WILL . . .**

....

....

SPACE: **ON MY MIND / IN MY HEART /
ON MY SHOULDERS / LIGHTING MY WAY . . .**

....

....

....

....

....

✷ ✷ ✷

ACCOMPLISHMENT: **TODAY, I ACHIEVED . . .**

....

....

CHALLENGE: **I WAS FACED WITH . . .**

....

....

GRATITUDE: **I'M GRATEFUL FOR . . .**

....

....

INTENTION: **TOMORROW I WILL . . .**

....

....

SPACE: **ON MY MIND / IN MY HEART /
ON MY SHOULDERS / LIGHTING MY WAY . . .**

....

....

....

....

....

✳ ✳ ✳

ACCOMPLISHMENT: **TODAY, I ACHIEVED . . .**

CHALLENGE: **I WAS FACED WITH . . .**

GRATITUDE: **I'M GRATEFUL FOR . . .**

INTENTION: **TOMORROW I WILL . . .**

SPACE: **ON MY MIND / IN MY HEART /
ON MY SHOULDERS / LIGHTING MY WAY . . .**

✳ ✳ ✳

ACCOMPLISHMENT: **TODAY, I ACHIEVED . . .**

- -

- -

CHALLENGE: **I WAS FACED WITH . . .**

- -

- -

GRATITUDE: **I'M GRATEFUL FOR . . .**

- -

- -

INTENTION: **TOMORROW I WILL . . .**

- -

- -

SPACE: **ON MY MIND / IN MY HEART /
ON MY SHOULDERS / LIGHTING MY WAY . . .**

- -

- -

- -

- -

"Working hard for something we don't care about is called stress: Working hard for something we love is called passion."

—SIMON SINEK

GRATEFUL FOR MEANINGFUL WORK

==

REWARDS
FOR EFFORT

REFLECTION

You spend a significant portion of your life working, and this time isn't lost. Your work, paid or unpaid, contributes to the entirety of your experience. The effort you put in can yield financial support for how you live your life, but that isn't the extent of the reward. Your paid or unpaid work supports your self-concept, passions, and values and can bring rich reward in many different ways to all the realms of your life.

SELF-INQUIRY INVITATIONS

* Reward doesn't mean being able to have everything you want. Instead, it refers to pursuing and attaining the things that align with your values. What material things do you enjoy because of your work? What nonmaterial things, such as love or passions, does your work allow you to cherish?
* What matters most to you in your life? Jot down what is important to you in all aspects of life, including work, family, community, spirituality, leisure, activity, and your sense of self.
* How does your work help you achieve what is important to you in other areas of your life?

✳ ✳ ✳

ACCOMPLISHMENT: **TODAY, I ACHIEVED . . .**

CHALLENGE: **I WAS FACED WITH . . .**

GRATITUDE: **I'M GRATEFUL FOR . . .**

INTENTION: **TOMORROW I WILL . . .**

SPACE: **ON MY MIND / IN MY HEART /
ON MY SHOULDERS / LIGHTING MY WAY . . .**

✳ ✳ ✳

ACCOMPLISHMENT: **TODAY, I ACHIEVED . . .**

....

....

CHALLENGE: **I WAS FACED WITH . . .**

....

....

GRATITUDE: **I'M GRATEFUL FOR . . .**

....

....

INTENTION: **TOMORROW I WILL . . .**

....

....

SPACE: **ON MY MIND / IN MY HEART /
ON MY SHOULDERS / LIGHTING MY WAY . . .**

....

....

....

....

....

✳ ✳ ✳

ACCOMPLISHMENT: **TODAY, I ACHIEVED . . .**

CHALLENGE: **I WAS FACED WITH . . .**

GRATITUDE: **I'M GRATEFUL FOR . . .**

INTENTION: **TOMORROW I WILL . . .**

SPACE: **ON MY MIND / IN MY HEART /
ON MY SHOULDERS / LIGHTING MY WAY . . .**

✳ ✳ ✳

ACCOMPLISHMENT: **TODAY, I ACHIEVED . . .**

CHALLENGE: **I WAS FACED WITH . . .**

GRATITUDE: **I'M GRATEFUL FOR . . .**

INTENTION: **TOMORROW I WILL . . .**

SPACE: **ON MY MIND / IN MY HEART /
ON MY SHOULDERS / LIGHTING MY WAY . . .**

✳ ✳ ✳

ACCOMPLISHMENT: **TODAY, I ACHIEVED . . .**

CHALLENGE: **I WAS FACED WITH . . .**

GRATITUDE: **I'M GRATEFUL FOR . . .**

INTENTION: **TOMORROW I WILL . . .**

SPACE: **ON MY MIND / IN MY HEART /
ON MY SHOULDERS / LIGHTING MY WAY . . .**

---

* * *

ACCOMPLISHMENT: **TODAY, I ACHIEVED . . .**

CHALLENGE: **I WAS FACED WITH . . .**

GRATITUDE: **I'M GRATEFUL FOR . . .**

INTENTION: **TOMORROW I WILL . . .**

SPACE: **ON MY MIND / IN MY HEART /
ON MY SHOULDERS / LIGHTING MY WAY . . .**

✳ ✳ ✳

ACCOMPLISHMENT: **TODAY, I ACHIEVED . . .**

CHALLENGE: **I WAS FACED WITH . . .**

GRATITUDE: **I'M GRATEFUL FOR . . .**

INTENTION: **TOMORROW I WILL . . .**

SPACE: **ON MY MIND / IN MY HEART /
ON MY SHOULDERS / LIGHTING MY WAY . . .**

✳ ✳ ✳

ACCOMPLISHMENT: **TODAY, I ACHIEVED . . .**

....

....

CHALLENGE: **I WAS FACED WITH . . .**

....

....

GRATITUDE: **I'M GRATEFUL FOR . . .**

....

....

INTENTION: **TOMORROW I WILL . . .**

....

....

SPACE: **ON MY MIND / IN MY HEART /
ON MY SHOULDERS / LIGHTING MY WAY . . .**

....

....

....

....

"The greatest act of courage is to be and to own all of who you are — without apology, without excuses, without masks to cover the truth of who you are."

—DEBBIE FORD

GRATEFUL FOR SOCIAL WELLBEING

AUTHENTIC
SELF

REFLECTION

Your authentic self is who you are at your core. It's the part of you that exists beyond the judgments and expectations imposed on you by others, such as your parents, teachers, partners, friends, and society in general. Your authentic self holds your deepest values, passions, hopes, dreams, and gifts. The strengths you have spring forth from your authentic self. Honoring who you truly are allows you to thrive, and it affects all your relationships and actions.

SELF-INQUIRY INVITATIONS

* Reflect on your thoughts, feelings, and actions today. When did you feel at your best, at ease, and most peaceful?
* Close your eyes and visualize yourself at your best. Now describe that best version of who you are.
* Think about what you say and how you act when you are with others. To what extent do your words and deeds align with your vision for yourself? What could you do differently to align with your authentic self more closely?
* What actions can you take tomorrow that will allow your best self to shine through?

ACCOMPLISHMENT: **TODAY, I ACHIEVED . . .**

CHALLENGE: **I WAS FACED WITH . . .**

GRATITUDE: **I'M GRATEFUL FOR . . .**

INTENTION: **TOMORROW I WILL . . .**

SPACE: **ON MY MIND / IN MY HEART /
ON MY SHOULDERS / LIGHTING MY WAY . . .**

✳ ✳ ✳

ACCOMPLISHMENT: **TODAY, I ACHIEVED . . .**

....

....

CHALLENGE: **I WAS FACED WITH . . .**

....

....

GRATITUDE: **I'M GRATEFUL FOR . . .**

....

....

INTENTION: **TOMORROW I WILL . . .**

....

....

SPACE: **ON MY MIND / IN MY HEART /
ON MY SHOULDERS / LIGHTING MY WAY . . .**

....

....

....

....

✳ ✳ ✳

ACCOMPLISHMENT: **TODAY, I ACHIEVED . . .**

CHALLENGE: **I WAS FACED WITH . . .**

GRATITUDE: **I'M GRATEFUL FOR . . .**

INTENTION: **TOMORROW I WILL . . .**

SPACE: **ON MY MIND / IN MY HEART /
ON MY SHOULDERS / LIGHTING MY WAY . . .**

✳ ✳ ✳

ACCOMPLISHMENT: **TODAY, I ACHIEVED . . .**

....

....

CHALLENGE: **I WAS FACED WITH . . .**

....

....

GRATITUDE: **I'M GRATEFUL FOR . . .**

....

....

INTENTION: **TOMORROW I WILL . . .**

....

....

SPACE: **ON MY MIND / IN MY HEART /
ON MY SHOULDERS / LIGHTING MY WAY . . .**

....

....

....

....

✳ ✳ ✳

ACCOMPLISHMENT: **TODAY, I ACHIEVED . . .**

CHALLENGE: **I WAS FACED WITH . . .**

GRATITUDE: **I'M GRATEFUL FOR . . .**

INTENTION: **TOMORROW I WILL . . .**

SPACE: **ON MY MIND / IN MY HEART /
ON MY SHOULDERS / LIGHTING MY WAY . . .**

* * *

ACCOMPLISHMENT: **TODAY, I ACHIEVED . . .**

....

....

CHALLENGE: **I WAS FACED WITH . . .**

....

....

GRATITUDE: **I'M GRATEFUL FOR . . .**

....

....

INTENTION: **TOMORROW I WILL . . .**

....

....

SPACE: **ON MY MIND / IN MY HEART /
ON MY SHOULDERS / LIGHTING MY WAY . . .**

....

....

....

....

....

✳ ✳ ✳

ACCOMPLISHMENT: TODAY, I ACHIEVED . . .

....

....

CHALLENGE: I WAS FACED WITH . . .

....

....

GRATITUDE: I'M GRATEFUL FOR . . .

....

....

INTENTION: TOMORROW I WILL . . .

....

....

SPACE: ON MY MIND / IN MY HEART /
ON MY SHOULDERS / LIGHTING MY WAY . . .

....

....

....

....

✳ ✳ ✳

ACCOMPLISHMENT: **TODAY, I ACHIEVED . . .**

....

....

CHALLENGE: **I WAS FACED WITH . . .**

....

....

GRATITUDE: **I'M GRATEFUL FOR . . .**

....

....

INTENTION: **TOMORROW I WILL . . .**

....

....

SPACE: **ON MY MIND / IN MY HEART /
ON MY SHOULDERS / LIGHTING MY WAY . . .**

....

....

....

....

"Each friend represents a world in us, a world possibly not born until they arrive, and it is only by this meeting that a new world is born."

—ANAÏS NIN

MEANINGFUL RELATIONSHIPS

REFLECTION

We all have a basic need to belong and to feel supported by others. Our need extends beyond mere connection for the sake of having contact, and it isn't the quantity of our relationships that matters. We need a small number of *meaningful* relationships where we feel safe, comfortable, and free to be our authentic selves. Research has repeatedly revealed that positive, healthy relationships contribute to mental and physical health, happiness, and a sense of meaning in life. Meaningful relationships, whether with a partner, family, friends, or coworkers, contribute tremendously to wellbeing.

SELF-INQUIRY INVITATIONS

✷ Meaningful relationships look a bit different for everyone. For you, what qualities make a relationship meaningful? How do you know if a relationship you are in is personally meaningful?

✷ A meaningful relationship does not mean a perfect relationship. What problems or faults are you willing to overlook to still consider a relationship meaningful?

✷ Reflect on the interactions you had today with someone important to you. How did your words and actions support this person? How did they support you?

✷ What is one goal you have for an important relationship in your life? How will you work toward this goal?

✳ ✳ ✳

ACCOMPLISHMENT: **TODAY, I ACHIEVED . . .**

CHALLENGE: **I WAS FACED WITH . . .**

GRATITUDE: **I'M GRATEFUL FOR . . .**

INTENTION: **TOMORROW I WILL . . .**

SPACE: **ON MY MIND / IN MY HEART /
ON MY SHOULDERS / LIGHTING MY WAY . . .**

✱ ✱ ✱

ACCOMPLISHMENT: **TODAY, I ACHIEVED . . .**

....

....

CHALLENGE: **I WAS FACED WITH . . .**

....

....

GRATITUDE: **I'M GRATEFUL FOR . . .**

....

....

INTENTION: **TOMORROW I WILL . . .**

....

....

SPACE: **ON MY MIND / IN MY HEART /
ON MY SHOULDERS / LIGHTING MY WAY . . .**

....

....

....

....

*** *** ***

ACCOMPLISHMENT: **TODAY, I ACHIEVED . . .**

....

....

CHALLENGE: **I WAS FACED WITH . . .**

....

....

GRATITUDE: **I'M GRATEFUL FOR . . .**

....

....

INTENTION: **TOMORROW I WILL . . .**

....

....

SPACE: **ON MY MIND / IN MY HEART /
ON MY SHOULDERS / LIGHTING MY WAY . . .**

....

....

....

....

✳ ✳ ✳

ACCOMPLISHMENT: **TODAY, I ACHIEVED . . .**

....

....

CHALLENGE: **I WAS FACED WITH . . .**

....

....

GRATITUDE: **I'M GRATEFUL FOR . . .**

....

....

INTENTION: **TOMORROW I WILL . . .**

....

....

SPACE: **ON MY MIND / IN MY HEART /
ON MY SHOULDERS / LIGHTING MY WAY . . .**

....

....

....

....

✳ ✳ ✳

ACCOMPLISHMENT: **TODAY, I ACHIEVED . . .**

....

....

CHALLENGE: **I WAS FACED WITH . . .**

....

....

GRATITUDE: **I'M GRATEFUL FOR . . .**

....

....

INTENTION: **TOMORROW I WILL . . .**

....

....

SPACE: **ON MY MIND / IN MY HEART /
ON MY SHOULDERS / LIGHTING MY WAY . . .**

....

....

....

....

✳ ✳ ✳

ACCOMPLISHMENT: **TODAY, I ACHIEVED . . .**

....

....

CHALLENGE: **I WAS FACED WITH . . .**

....

....

GRATITUDE: **I'M GRATEFUL FOR . . .**

....

....

INTENTION: **TOMORROW I WILL . . .**

....

....

SPACE: **ON MY MIND / IN MY HEART /
ON MY SHOULDERS / LIGHTING MY WAY . . .**

....

....

....

....

✳ ✳ ✳

ACCOMPLISHMENT: **TODAY, I ACHIEVED . . .**

CHALLENGE: **I WAS FACED WITH . . .**

GRATITUDE: **I'M GRATEFUL FOR . . .**

INTENTION: **TOMORROW I WILL . . .**

SPACE: **ON MY MIND / IN MY HEART /
ON MY SHOULDERS / LIGHTING MY WAY . . .**

✳ ✳ ✳

ACCOMPLISHMENT: **TODAY, I ACHIEVED . . .**

CHALLENGE: **I WAS FACED WITH . . .**

GRATITUDE: **I'M GRATEFUL FOR . . .**

INTENTION: **TOMORROW I WILL . . .**

SPACE: **ON MY MIND / IN MY HEART /
ON MY SHOULDERS / LIGHTING MY WAY . . .**

"We cannot do life alone and expect to keep mentally, emotionally, and spiritually healthy. Everyone needs some sort of support system on which to rely."

—RICHELLE E. GOODRICH

GRATEFUL FOR SOCIAL WELLBEING

SOCIAL SUPPORT NETWORK

REFLECTION

Social networks aren't just for the gregarious extroverts among us. A healthy social support network can mean having a few people with whom you share the ups and downs of life in simple ways. Your network is made up of the friends, family members, coworkers, neighbors, and acquaintances with whom you share laughter, tears, and even boredom. They're the people who help you survive stressors big and small and with whom you share your joys and celebrate your triumphs.

SELF-INQUIRY INVITATIONS

* Who do you enjoy occasional conversations with? How can you connect with them more often?
* Who has helped you through a challenging situation lately? In what ways do you let them know you appreciate them?
* Think of people in your life and how they affect your energy. Who would you like to spend more time with, and who would you like to spend less?
* How do the people in your life make the mundane and often stressful tasks of daily living a little better and your mood brighter?

✳ ✳ ✳

ACCOMPLISHMENT: **TODAY, I ACHIEVED . . .**

....

....

CHALLENGE: **I WAS FACED WITH . . .**

....

....

GRATITUDE: **I'M GRATEFUL FOR . . .**

....

....

INTENTION: **TOMORROW I WILL . . .**

....

....

SPACE: **ON MY MIND / IN MY HEART /
ON MY SHOULDERS / LIGHTING MY WAY . . .**

....

....

....

....

....

✳ ✳ ✳

ACCOMPLISHMENT: **TODAY, I ACHIEVED . . .**

....

....

CHALLENGE: **I WAS FACED WITH . . .**

....

....

GRATITUDE: **I'M GRATEFUL FOR . . .**

....

....

INTENTION: **TOMORROW I WILL . . .**

....

....

SPACE: **ON MY MIND / IN MY HEART /
ON MY SHOULDERS / LIGHTING MY WAY . . .**

....

....

....

....

✳ ✳ ✳

ACCOMPLISHMENT: **TODAY, I ACHIEVED . . .**

....

....

CHALLENGE: **I WAS FACED WITH . . .**

....

....

GRATITUDE: **I'M GRATEFUL FOR . . .**

....

....

INTENTION: **TOMORROW I WILL . . .**

....

....

SPACE: **ON MY MIND / IN MY HEART /
ON MY SHOULDERS / LIGHTING MY WAY . . .**

....

....

....

....

....

✳ ✳ ✳

ACCOMPLISHMENT: **TODAY, I ACHIEVED . . .**

....

....

CHALLENGE: **I WAS FACED WITH . . .**

....

....

GRATITUDE: **I'M GRATEFUL FOR . . .**

....

....

INTENTION: **TOMORROW I WILL . . .**

....

....

SPACE: **ON MY MIND / IN MY HEART /
ON MY SHOULDERS / LIGHTING MY WAY . . .**

....

....

....

....

....

* * *

ACCOMPLISHMENT: **TODAY, I ACHIEVED . . .**

....

....

CHALLENGE: **I WAS FACED WITH . . .**

....

....

GRATITUDE: **I'M GRATEFUL FOR . . .**

....

....

INTENTION: **TOMORROW I WILL . . .**

....

....

SPACE: **ON MY MIND / IN MY HEART /
ON MY SHOULDERS / LIGHTING MY WAY . . .**

....

....

....

....

....

✳ ✳ ✳

ACCOMPLISHMENT: **TODAY, I ACHIEVED . . .**

....

....

CHALLENGE: **I WAS FACED WITH . . .**

....

....

GRATITUDE: **I'M GRATEFUL FOR . . .**

....

....

INTENTION: **TOMORROW I WILL . . .**

....

....

SPACE: **ON MY MIND / IN MY HEART /
ON MY SHOULDERS / LIGHTING MY WAY . . .**

....

....

....

....

ACCOMPLISHMENT: **TODAY, I ACHIEVED . . .**

....

....

CHALLENGE: **I WAS FACED WITH . . .**

....

....

GRATITUDE: **I'M GRATEFUL FOR . . .**

....

....

INTENTION: **TOMORROW I WILL . . .**

....

....

SPACE: **ON MY MIND / IN MY HEART /
ON MY SHOULDERS / LIGHTING MY WAY . . .**

....

....

....

....

....

✳ ✳ ✳

ACCOMPLISHMENT: **TODAY, I ACHIEVED . . .**

....

....

CHALLENGE: **I WAS FACED WITH . . .**

....

....

GRATITUDE: **I'M GRATEFUL FOR . . .**

....

....

INTENTION: **TOMORROW I WILL . . .**

....

....

SPACE: **ON MY MIND / IN MY HEART /
ON MY SHOULDERS / LIGHTING MY WAY . . .**

....

....

....

....

"Money never made a man happy yet, nor will it. The more a man has, the more he wants. Instead of filling a vacuum, it makes one."

—BENJAMIN FRANKLIN

GRATEFUL FOR FINANCIAL WISDOM

NEEDS
VERSUS
WANTS

REFLECTION

Both wants and needs are important in the scheme of our total well-being, but not equally so. Needs are required for health and safety. An absence of any need is harmful. Wants are things that make you feel more pleased. The absence of a want might be disappointing, but it isn't dangerous. Being intentional about determining which expenses are necessary and which are desires allows you to be more confident in your spending, decrease financial anxiety, and increase equanimity.

SELF-INQUIRY INVITATIONS

* Do you have to spend money to meet your higher-level requirements like self-esteem, respect, belonging, and becoming your most authentic self? How might you pursue these without huge financial expense?
* "Needs" and "wants" are highly personal. Make a list of your own needs and wants, then honestly evaluate them, moving items between the categories.
* Tap into your inner creativity. In what ways can you meet your life needs by spending a little less? Could you change where you shop or drive less? Can you make a game out of challenging yourself to think outside of the wallet?

✳ ✳ ✳

ACCOMPLISHMENT: **TODAY, I ACHIEVED . . .**

....

....

CHALLENGE: **I WAS FACED WITH . . .**

....

....

GRATITUDE: **I'M GRATEFUL FOR . . .**

....

....

INTENTION: **TOMORROW I WILL . . .**

....

....

SPACE: **ON MY MIND / IN MY HEART /
ON MY SHOULDERS / LIGHTING MY WAY . . .**

....

....

....

....

....

ACCOMPLISHMENT: **TODAY, I ACHIEVED . . .**

....

....

CHALLENGE: **I WAS FACED WITH . . .**

....

....

GRATITUDE: **I'M GRATEFUL FOR . . .**

....

....

INTENTION: **TOMORROW I WILL . . .**

....

....

SPACE: **ON MY MIND / IN MY HEART /
ON MY SHOULDERS / LIGHTING MY WAY . . .**

....

....

....

....

....

✳ ✳ ✳

ACCOMPLISHMENT: **TODAY, I ACHIEVED . . .**

....

....

CHALLENGE: **I WAS FACED WITH . . .**

....

....

GRATITUDE: **I'M GRATEFUL FOR . . .**

....

....

INTENTION: **TOMORROW I WILL . . .**

....

....

SPACE: **ON MY MIND / IN MY HEART /
ON MY SHOULDERS / LIGHTING MY WAY . . .**

....

....

....

....

✳ ✳ ✳

ACCOMPLISHMENT: **TODAY, I ACHIEVED . . .**

....

....

CHALLENGE: **I WAS FACED WITH . . .**

....

....

GRATITUDE: **I'M GRATEFUL FOR . . .**

....

....

INTENTION: **TOMORROW I WILL . . .**

....

....

SPACE: **ON MY MIND / IN MY HEART /
ON MY SHOULDERS / LIGHTING MY WAY . . .**

....

....

....

....

....

✳ ✳ ✳

ACCOMPLISHMENT: **TODAY, I ACHIEVED . . .**

....

....

CHALLENGE: **I WAS FACED WITH . . .**

....

....

GRATITUDE: **I'M GRATEFUL FOR . . .**

....

....

INTENTION: **TOMORROW I WILL . . .**

....

....

SPACE: **ON MY MIND / IN MY HEART /
ON MY SHOULDERS / LIGHTING MY WAY . . .**

....

....

....

....

✳ ✳ ✳

ACCOMPLISHMENT: **TODAY, I ACHIEVED . . .**

CHALLENGE: **I WAS FACED WITH . . .**

GRATITUDE: **I'M GRATEFUL FOR . . .**

INTENTION: **TOMORROW I WILL . . .**

SPACE: **ON MY MIND / IN MY HEART /
ON MY SHOULDERS / LIGHTING MY WAY . . .**

✳ ✳ ✳

ACCOMPLISHMENT: **TODAY, I ACHIEVED . . .**

....

....

CHALLENGE: **I WAS FACED WITH . . .**

....

....

GRATITUDE: **I'M GRATEFUL FOR . . .**

....

....

INTENTION: **TOMORROW I WILL . . .**

....

....

SPACE: **ON MY MIND / IN MY HEART /
ON MY SHOULDERS / LIGHTING MY WAY . . .**

....

....

....

....

....

✷ ✷ ✷

ACCOMPLISHMENT: **TODAY, I ACHIEVED . . .**

CHALLENGE: **I WAS FACED WITH . . .**

GRATITUDE: **I'M GRATEFUL FOR . . .**

INTENTION: **TOMORROW I WILL . . .**

SPACE: **ON MY MIND / IN MY HEART /
ON MY SHOULDERS / LIGHTING MY WAY . . .**

"*The desire of gold is not for gold. It is for the means of freedom and benefit.*"

—RALPH WALDO EMERSON

GRATEFUL FOR FINANCIAL WISDOM

SPENDING MINDFULLY

REFLECTION

Financial mindfulness is a unique relationship you create with your money. Being mindful of money involves pausing and reflecting on how and why you are spending your resources. Awareness of present-moment spending helps ease anxiety and money worries because you're attuned to your current situation and how it fits in to your life goals, allowing you to remain calm and focused for optimal financial decisions, one moment at a time.

SELF-INQUIRY INVITATIONS

✳ How does your inner experience influence your spending? In thinking about your buying habits, what patterns exist between spending and thoughts, emotions, hunger, thirst, fatigue, and boredom?

✳ What would it be like to pause for a day (or more) before finalizing purchases that fall into the "want" category? What would you have to lose by delaying spending? What would you have to gain?

✳ List some purchases you've been wanting to make. What is driving your desire? In what ways would spending money on them move you toward your greater life goals and values? In what ways would these expenditures impede your progress?

✳ ✳ ✳

ACCOMPLISHMENT: **TODAY, I ACHIEVED . . .**

CHALLENGE: **I WAS FACED WITH . . .**

GRATITUDE: **I'M GRATEFUL FOR . . .**

INTENTION: **TOMORROW I WILL . . .**

SPACE: **ON MY MIND / IN MY HEART /
ON MY SHOULDERS / LIGHTING MY WAY . . .**

✳ ✳ ✳

ACCOMPLISHMENT: **TODAY, I ACHIEVED . . .**

....

....

CHALLENGE: **I WAS FACED WITH . . .**

....

....

GRATITUDE: **I'M GRATEFUL FOR . . .**

....

....

INTENTION: **TOMORROW I WILL . . .**

....

....

SPACE: **ON MY MIND / IN MY HEART /
ON MY SHOULDERS / LIGHTING MY WAY . . .**

....

....

....

....

✳ ✳ ✳

ACCOMPLISHMENT: **TODAY, I ACHIEVED . . .**

CHALLENGE: **I WAS FACED WITH . . .**

GRATITUDE: **I'M GRATEFUL FOR . . .**

INTENTION: **TOMORROW I WILL . . .**

SPACE: **ON MY MIND / IN MY HEART /
ON MY SHOULDERS / LIGHTING MY WAY . . .**

✳ ✳ ✳

ACCOMPLISHMENT: **TODAY, I ACHIEVED . . .**

CHALLENGE: **I WAS FACED WITH . . .**

GRATITUDE: **I'M GRATEFUL FOR . . .**

INTENTION: **TOMORROW I WILL . . .**

SPACE: **ON MY MIND / IN MY HEART /
ON MY SHOULDERS / LIGHTING MY WAY . . .**

✶ ✶ ✶

ACCOMPLISHMENT: **TODAY, I ACHIEVED . . .**

....

....

CHALLENGE: **I WAS FACED WITH . . .**

....

....

GRATITUDE: **I'M GRATEFUL FOR . . .**

....

....

INTENTION: **TOMORROW I WILL . . .**

....

....

SPACE: **ON MY MIND / IN MY HEART /
ON MY SHOULDERS / LIGHTING MY WAY . . .**

....

....

....

....

✳ ✳ ✳

ACCOMPLISHMENT: **TODAY, I ACHIEVED . . .**

....

....

CHALLENGE: **I WAS FACED WITH . . .**

....

....

GRATITUDE: **I'M GRATEFUL FOR . . .**

....

....

INTENTION: **TOMORROW I WILL . . .**

....

....

SPACE: **ON MY MIND / IN MY HEART /
ON MY SHOULDERS / LIGHTING MY WAY . . .**

....

....

....

....

✳ ✳ ✳

ACCOMPLISHMENT: **TODAY, I ACHIEVED . . .**

....

....

CHALLENGE: **I WAS FACED WITH . . .**

....

....

GRATITUDE: **I'M GRATEFUL FOR . . .**

....

....

INTENTION: **TOMORROW I WILL . . .**

....

....

SPACE: **ON MY MIND / IN MY HEART /
ON MY SHOULDERS / LIGHTING MY WAY . . .**

....

....

....

....

✳ ✳ ✳

ACCOMPLISHMENT: **TODAY, I ACHIEVED . . .**

....

....

CHALLENGE: **I WAS FACED WITH . . .**

....

....

GRATITUDE: **I'M GRATEFUL FOR . . .**

....

....

INTENTION: **TOMORROW I WILL . . .**

....

....

SPACE: **ON MY MIND / IN MY HEART /
ON MY SHOULDERS / LIGHTING MY WAY . . .**

....

....

....

....

"How we behave toward our money, how we treat our money, speaks volumes about how we perceive and value ourselves."

—SUZE ORMAN

GRATEFUL FOR FINANCIAL WISDOM

SAVING FOR FUTURE GOALS

REFLECTION

Wise spending and financial saving are ultimately about ensuring that your needs are met now and into the future. Take charge of your long-term safety, security, health, and happiness by using these needs as guiding beacons. Establishing short-term, midterm, and long-term goals that align with what is important to you can help you spend mindfully and adjust your money habits. Rather than being driven by emotional impulses, you'll be led by intentional saving for meaningful life goals.

SELF-INQUIRY INVITATIONS

* What does "financial security" mean for you? When you envision yourself 10, 20, 30, or more years from now, what resources will you need to be sheltered, fed, healthy, socially connected, and satisfied with yourself?
* Consider your current spending. What are you willing to forgo now in order to enjoy financial security in your future?
* Saving for the future can involve cutting back on spending as well as bringing in money. Do you have unnecessary possessions you could sell? What about a hobby or passion you could monetize? Brainstorm creative ways to bring in a little extra cash to pad your savings account.

✲ ✴ ✲

ACCOMPLISHMENT: **TODAY, I ACHIEVED . . .**

....

....

CHALLENGE: **I WAS FACED WITH . . .**

....

....

GRATITUDE: **I'M GRATEFUL FOR . . .**

....

....

INTENTION: **TOMORROW I WILL . . .**

....

....

SPACE: **ON MY MIND / IN MY HEART /
ON MY SHOULDERS / LIGHTING MY WAY . . .**

....

....

....

....

✳ ✳ ✳

ACCOMPLISHMENT: **TODAY, I ACHIEVED . . .**

CHALLENGE: **I WAS FACED WITH . . .**

GRATITUDE: **I'M GRATEFUL FOR . . .**

INTENTION: **TOMORROW I WILL . . .**

SPACE: **ON MY MIND / IN MY HEART /**
ON MY SHOULDERS / LIGHTING MY WAY . . .

✳ ✳ ✳

ACCOMPLISHMENT: **TODAY, I ACHIEVED . . .**

CHALLENGE: **I WAS FACED WITH . . .**

GRATITUDE: **I'M GRATEFUL FOR . . .**

INTENTION: **TOMORROW I WILL . . .**

SPACE: **ON MY MIND / IN MY HEART /
ON MY SHOULDERS / LIGHTING MY WAY . . .**

✳ ✳ ✳

ACCOMPLISHMENT: **TODAY, I ACHIEVED . . .**

CHALLENGE: **I WAS FACED WITH . . .**

GRATITUDE: **I'M GRATEFUL FOR . . .**

INTENTION: **TOMORROW I WILL . . .**

SPACE: **ON MY MIND / IN MY HEART /
ON MY SHOULDERS / LIGHTING MY WAY . . .**

✲ ✲ ✲

ACCOMPLISHMENT: **TODAY, I ACHIEVED . . .**

CHALLENGE: **I WAS FACED WITH . . .**

GRATITUDE: **I'M GRATEFUL FOR . . .**

INTENTION: **TOMORROW I WILL . . .**

SPACE: **ON MY MIND / IN MY HEART /
ON MY SHOULDERS / LIGHTING MY WAY . . .**

✷ ✷ ✷

ACCOMPLISHMENT: **TODAY, I ACHIEVED . . .**

....

....

CHALLENGE: **I WAS FACED WITH . . .**

....

....

GRATITUDE: **I'M GRATEFUL FOR . . .**

....

....

INTENTION: **TOMORROW I WILL . . .**

....

....

SPACE: **ON MY MIND / IN MY HEART /
ON MY SHOULDERS / LIGHTING MY WAY . . .**

....

....

....

....

....

✳ ✳ ✳

ACCOMPLISHMENT: **TODAY, I ACHIEVED . . .**

CHALLENGE: **I WAS FACED WITH . . .**

GRATITUDE: **I'M GRATEFUL FOR . . .**

INTENTION: **TOMORROW I WILL . . .**

SPACE: **ON MY MIND / IN MY HEART /
ON MY SHOULDERS / LIGHTING MY WAY . . .**

✷ ✷ ✷

ACCOMPLISHMENT: **TODAY, I ACHIEVED . . .**

....

....

CHALLENGE: **I WAS FACED WITH . . .**

....

....

GRATITUDE: **I'M GRATEFUL FOR . . .**

....

....

INTENTION: **TOMORROW I WILL . . .**

....

....

SPACE: **ON MY MIND / IN MY HEART /
ON MY SHOULDERS / LIGHTING MY WAY . . .**

....

....

....

....

"*If only one thing is healed in your life, it should be the separation between mind and body.*"

—DEEPAK CHOPRA AND RUDOLPH E. TANZI,
THE HEALING SELF

GRATEFUL FOR MY BODY

HEALTH AND MOOD

REFLECTION

Researchers continue to discover just how complex and intimate the relationship is between mental and physical health. Our bodies respond directly to our thoughts and feelings; likewise, our thoughts and feelings are influenced by happenings in our body. This means, of course, that we can help our minds and bodies work for each other rather than against each other. By purposefully nurturing both mind and body, you can boost your health and your mood every day.

SELF-INQUIRY INVITATIONS

✶ Recall a recent emotional experience, positive or negative. Allow yourself to visualize it fully, remembering the feeling. Where in your body do you notice the emotion? How can you nurture your body there?

✶ Remember a time when you felt physical pain or illness. How was your mood? What thoughts and feelings did you have at the time?

✶ Habits influence mood. Exercise, nutrition, relaxation, mindfulness, pursuing passions, fostering social connections, and cultivating a positive outlook contribute to physical and emotional wellness. What one habit might you improve as you continue your journey to total wellbeing? List action steps to take tomorrow.

* * *

ACCOMPLISHMENT: **TODAY, I ACHIEVED . . .**

CHALLENGE: **I WAS FACED WITH . . .**

GRATITUDE: **I'M GRATEFUL FOR . . .**

INTENTION: **TOMORROW I WILL . . .**

SPACE: **ON MY MIND / IN MY HEART /
ON MY SHOULDERS / LIGHTING MY WAY . . .**

✳ ✳ ✳

ACCOMPLISHMENT: **TODAY, I ACHIEVED . . .**

CHALLENGE: **I WAS FACED WITH . . .**

GRATITUDE: **I'M GRATEFUL FOR . . .**

INTENTION: **TOMORROW I WILL . . .**

SPACE: **ON MY MIND / IN MY HEART /
ON MY SHOULDERS / LIGHTING MY WAY . . .**

✷ ✷ ✷

ACCOMPLISHMENT: **TODAY, I ACHIEVED . . .**

CHALLENGE: **I WAS FACED WITH . . .**

GRATITUDE: **I'M GRATEFUL FOR . . .**

INTENTION: **TOMORROW I WILL . . .**

SPACE: **ON MY MIND / IN MY HEART /
ON MY SHOULDERS / LIGHTING MY WAY . . .**

ACCOMPLISHMENT: **TODAY, I ACHIEVED . . .**

CHALLENGE: **I WAS FACED WITH . . .**

GRATITUDE: **I'M GRATEFUL FOR . . .**

INTENTION: **TOMORROW I WILL . . .**

SPACE: **ON MY MIND / IN MY HEART /
ON MY SHOULDERS / LIGHTING MY WAY . . .**

✳ ✳ ✳

ACCOMPLISHMENT: **TODAY, I ACHIEVED . . .**

....

....

CHALLENGE: **I WAS FACED WITH . . .**

....

....

GRATITUDE: **I'M GRATEFUL FOR . . .**

....

....

INTENTION: **TOMORROW I WILL . . .**

....

....

SPACE: **ON MY MIND / IN MY HEART /
ON MY SHOULDERS / LIGHTING MY WAY . . .**

....

....

....

....

✳ ✳ ✳

ACCOMPLISHMENT: **TODAY, I ACHIEVED . . .**

CHALLENGE: **I WAS FACED WITH . . .**

GRATITUDE: **I'M GRATEFUL FOR . . .**

INTENTION: **TOMORROW I WILL . . .**

SPACE: **ON MY MIND / IN MY HEART /
ON MY SHOULDERS / LIGHTING MY WAY . . .**

ACCOMPLISHMENT: **TODAY, I ACHIEVED . . .**

CHALLENGE: **I WAS FACED WITH . . .**

GRATITUDE: **I'M GRATEFUL FOR . . .**

INTENTION: **TOMORROW I WILL . . .**

SPACE: **ON MY MIND / IN MY HEART / ON MY SHOULDERS / LIGHTING MY WAY . . .**

✳ ✳ ✳

ACCOMPLISHMENT: **TODAY, I ACHIEVED . . .**

....

....

CHALLENGE: **I WAS FACED WITH . . .**

....

....

GRATITUDE: **I'M GRATEFUL FOR . . .**

....

....

INTENTION: **TOMORROW I WILL . . .**

....

....

SPACE: **ON MY MIND / IN MY HEART /
ON MY SHOULDERS / LIGHTING MY WAY . . .**

....

....

....

....

"Since I don't look like every other girl, it takes a while to be okay with that. To be different. But different is good."

—SERENA WILLIAMS

GRATEFUL FOR MY BODY

BODY IMAGE

REFLECTION

Body image isn't about how the world sees us. It's about how we perceive ourselves. It involves the thoughts and feelings we have about our body and the actions we take because of these things. The human brain has a negativity bias that extends to our perceptions, thoughts, and feelings about our own bodies. Recognizing and replacing negative body beliefs is connected to enhanced self-acceptance and confidence.

SELF-INQUIRY INVITATIONS

* Focus on all that your body can do and has done for you. Express gratitude for your body, appreciating and thanking all the different components and how they help you live your life.
* It's okay to have health-related goals—just remember that how you frame them matters to your wellbeing, too. Think of a goal you have related to your body. Write it here, taking care to word it to capture what you *do* want rather than what you *don't*. ("I don't want to be in pain" might become "I will stretch gently and rest my body so it feels better.")
* Stand in front of a mirror and study your face and your body. Write a description of all the beauty you see in yourself.

✳ ✳ ✳

ACCOMPLISHMENT: **TODAY, I ACHIEVED . . .**

....

....

CHALLENGE: **I WAS FACED WITH . . .**

....

....

GRATITUDE: **I'M GRATEFUL FOR . . .**

....

....

INTENTION: **TOMORROW I WILL . . .**

....

....

SPACE: **ON MY MIND / IN MY HEART /
ON MY SHOULDERS / LIGHTING MY WAY . . .**

....

....

....

....

✳ ✳ ✳

ACCOMPLISHMENT: **TODAY, I ACHIEVED . . .**

....

....

CHALLENGE: **I WAS FACED WITH . . .**

....

....

GRATITUDE: **I'M GRATEFUL FOR . . .**

....

....

INTENTION: **TOMORROW I WILL . . .**

....

....

SPACE: **ON MY MIND / IN MY HEART /
ON MY SHOULDERS / LIGHTING MY WAY . . .**

....

....

....

....

....

✳ ✳ ✳

ACCOMPLISHMENT: **TODAY, I ACHIEVED . . .**

CHALLENGE: **I WAS FACED WITH . . .**

GRATITUDE: **I'M GRATEFUL FOR . . .**

INTENTION: **TOMORROW I WILL . . .**

SPACE: **ON MY MIND / IN MY HEART /
ON MY SHOULDERS / LIGHTING MY WAY . . .**

***

ACCOMPLISHMENT: **TODAY, I ACHIEVED . . .**

....

....

CHALLENGE: **I WAS FACED WITH . . .**

....

....

GRATITUDE: **I'M GRATEFUL FOR . . .**

....

....

INTENTION: **TOMORROW I WILL . . .**

....

....

SPACE: **ON MY MIND / IN MY HEART /
ON MY SHOULDERS / LIGHTING MY WAY . . .**

....

....

....

....

✳ ✳ ✳

ACCOMPLISHMENT: **TODAY, I ACHIEVED . . .**

....

....

CHALLENGE: **I WAS FACED WITH . . .**

....

....

GRATITUDE: **I'M GRATEFUL FOR . . .**

....

....

INTENTION: **TOMORROW I WILL . . .**

....

....

SPACE: **ON MY MIND / IN MY HEART /
ON MY SHOULDERS / LIGHTING MY WAY . . .**

....

....

....

....

✳ ✳ ✳

ACCOMPLISHMENT: **TODAY, I ACHIEVED . . .**

CHALLENGE: **I WAS FACED WITH . . .**

GRATITUDE: **I'M GRATEFUL FOR . . .**

INTENTION: **TOMORROW I WILL . . .**

SPACE: **ON MY MIND / IN MY HEART /
ON MY SHOULDERS / LIGHTING MY WAY . . .**

✳ ✳ ✳

ACCOMPLISHMENT: **TODAY, I ACHIEVED . . .**

....

....

CHALLENGE: **I WAS FACED WITH . . .**

....

....

GRATITUDE: **I'M GRATEFUL FOR . . .**

....

....

INTENTION: **TOMORROW I WILL . . .**

....

....

SPACE: **ON MY MIND / IN MY HEART /
ON MY SHOULDERS / LIGHTING MY WAY . . .**

....

....

....

....

✳ ✳ ✳

ACCOMPLISHMENT: **TODAY, I ACHIEVED . . .**

. . . .

. . . .

CHALLENGE: **I WAS FACED WITH . . .**

. . . .

. . . .

GRATITUDE: **I'M GRATEFUL FOR . . .**

. . . .

. . . .

INTENTION: **TOMORROW I WILL . . .**

. . . .

. . . .

SPACE: **ON MY MIND / IN MY HEART /
ON MY SHOULDERS / LIGHTING MY WAY . . .**

. . . .

. . . .

. . . .

. . . .

"Health is hearty, health is harmony, health is happiness."

—AMIT KALANTRI

GRATEFUL FOR MY BODY

GETTING STRONGER

REFLECTION

You know the importance of nutrition, exercise, sleep, and stress management. Now it's time to get personal. The key to growing mentally and physically stronger is to tune in deeply and frequently to *your* body. Rather than following generic lists of recommendations, learn to listen and respond to what you need moment by moment, and notice how doing this makes you even stronger.

SELF-INQUIRY INVITATIONS

* What does physical strength mean to you? What will you be able to do when you are feeling stronger?
* Make a habit of pausing to ask yourself what you need in this moment to be strong right now. Practice this here. Is your body exhausted and in need of rest? Do your brain and muscles need movement or nourishment? Describe how you are feeling and how you can nurture yourself.
* Do you have a healthy habit you've been meaning to develop? Is your body asking you to do this to help it feel stronger? How will you honor that tomorrow?

✳ ✳ ✳

ACCOMPLISHMENT: **TODAY, I ACHIEVED . . .**

....

....

CHALLENGE: **I WAS FACED WITH . . .**

....

....

GRATITUDE: **I'M GRATEFUL FOR . . .**

....

....

INTENTION: **TOMORROW I WILL . . .**

....

....

SPACE: **ON MY MIND / IN MY HEART /
ON MY SHOULDERS / LIGHTING MY WAY . . .**

....

....

....

....

....

✷ ✷ ✷

ACCOMPLISHMENT: **TODAY, I ACHIEVED . . .**

....

....

CHALLENGE: **I WAS FACED WITH . . .**

....

....

GRATITUDE: **I'M GRATEFUL FOR . . .**

....

....

INTENTION: **TOMORROW I WILL . . .**

....

....

SPACE: **ON MY MIND / IN MY HEART /
ON MY SHOULDERS / LIGHTING MY WAY . . .**

....

....

....

....

....

✳ ✳ ✳

ACCOMPLISHMENT: **TODAY, I ACHIEVED . . .**

....

....

CHALLENGE: **I WAS FACED WITH . . .**

....

....

GRATITUDE: **I'M GRATEFUL FOR . . .**

....

....

INTENTION: **TOMORROW I WILL . . .**

....

....

SPACE: **ON MY MIND / IN MY HEART /
ON MY SHOULDERS / LIGHTING MY WAY . . .**

....

....

....

....

....

✳ ✳ ✳

ACCOMPLISHMENT: **TODAY, I ACHIEVED . . .**

CHALLENGE: **I WAS FACED WITH . . .**

GRATITUDE: **I'M GRATEFUL FOR . . .**

INTENTION: **TOMORROW I WILL . . .**

SPACE: **ON MY MIND / IN MY HEART /
ON MY SHOULDERS / LIGHTING MY WAY . . .**

✳ ✳ ✳

ACCOMPLISHMENT: **TODAY, I ACHIEVED . . .**

CHALLENGE: **I WAS FACED WITH . . .**

GRATITUDE: **I'M GRATEFUL FOR . . .**

INTENTION: **TOMORROW I WILL . . .**

SPACE: **ON MY MIND / IN MY HEART /
ON MY SHOULDERS / LIGHTING MY WAY . . .**

✳ ✳ ✳

ACCOMPLISHMENT: **TODAY, I ACHIEVED . . .**

....

....

CHALLENGE: **I WAS FACED WITH . . .**

....

....

GRATITUDE: **I'M GRATEFUL FOR . . .**

....

....

INTENTION: **TOMORROW I WILL . . .**

....

....

SPACE: **ON MY MIND / IN MY HEART /
ON MY SHOULDERS / LIGHTING MY WAY . . .**

....

....

....

....

*** *** ***

ACCOMPLISHMENT: **TODAY, I ACHIEVED . . .**

CHALLENGE: **I WAS FACED WITH . . .**

GRATITUDE: **I'M GRATEFUL FOR . . .**

INTENTION: **TOMORROW I WILL . . .**

SPACE: **ON MY MIND / IN MY HEART /
ON MY SHOULDERS / LIGHTING MY WAY . . .**

✱ ✱ ✱

ACCOMPLISHMENT: **TODAY, I ACHIEVED . . .**

....

....

CHALLENGE: **I WAS FACED WITH . . .**

....

....

GRATITUDE: **I'M GRATEFUL FOR . . .**

....

....

INTENTION: **TOMORROW I WILL . . .**

....

....

SPACE: **ON MY MIND / IN MY HEART /
ON MY SHOULDERS / LIGHTING MY WAY . . .**

....

....

....

....

"And perhaps the best answer is not to tolerate differences, not even to accept them. But to celebrate them. Maybe then those who are different would feel more loved, and less, well, tolerated."

—BILL KONIGSBERG

VALUING
DIVERSITY

REFLECTION

The human species is wonderfully exciting and varied, composed of billions of unique individuals, each and every one bringing their unparalleled looks, ideas, perspectives, talents, skills, and strengths to our interconnected world. You are among this thrilling throng. Imagine what a world this would be if we focused on each person's noteworthy strengths. When we see each other, and ourselves, for what we contribute, loving-kindness, growth, and positive daily experiences dominate.

SELF-INQUIRY INVITATIONS

* Reflect on when you felt your best today. What were you thinking, feeling, and doing? What does this say about what you have to contribute to those around you?
* In what ways could you expand your offerings to include people you might not regularly interact with?
* Practice spotting the good in others, especially those you may not fully understand. Think about someone different from you, and jot down strengths, talents, or skills you've observed but may not have appreciated fully.

＊ ＊ ＊

ACCOMPLISHMENT: **TODAY, I ACHIEVED . . .**

....

....

CHALLENGE: **I WAS FACED WITH . . .**

....

....

GRATITUDE: **I'M GRATEFUL FOR . . .**

....

....

INTENTION: **TOMORROW I WILL . . .**

....

....

SPACE: **ON MY MIND / IN MY HEART /
ON MY SHOULDERS / LIGHTING MY WAY . . .**

....

....

....

....

....

✳ ✳ ✳

ACCOMPLISHMENT: **TODAY, I ACHIEVED . . .**

....

....

CHALLENGE: **I WAS FACED WITH . . .**

....

....

GRATITUDE: **I'M GRATEFUL FOR . . .**

....

....

INTENTION: **TOMORROW I WILL . . .**

....

....

SPACE: **ON MY MIND / IN MY HEART /
ON MY SHOULDERS / LIGHTING MY WAY . . .**

....

....

....

....

....

✳ ✳ ✳

ACCOMPLISHMENT: **TODAY, I ACHIEVED . . .**

....

....

CHALLENGE: **I WAS FACED WITH . . .**

....

....

GRATITUDE: **I'M GRATEFUL FOR . . .**

....

....

INTENTION: **TOMORROW I WILL . . .**

....

....

SPACE: **ON MY MIND / IN MY HEART /
ON MY SHOULDERS / LIGHTING MY WAY . . .**

....

....

....

....

✳ ✳ ✳

ACCOMPLISHMENT: **TODAY, I ACHIEVED . . .**

....

....

CHALLENGE: **I WAS FACED WITH . . .**

....

....

GRATITUDE: **I'M GRATEFUL FOR . . .**

....

....

INTENTION: **TOMORROW I WILL . . .**

....

....

SPACE: **ON MY MIND / IN MY HEART /
ON MY SHOULDERS / LIGHTING MY WAY . . .**

....

....

....

....

✳ ✳ ✳

ACCOMPLISHMENT: **TODAY, I ACHIEVED . . .**

CHALLENGE: **I WAS FACED WITH . . .**

GRATITUDE: **I'M GRATEFUL FOR . . .**

INTENTION: **TOMORROW I WILL . . .**

SPACE: **ON MY MIND / IN MY HEART /
ON MY SHOULDERS / LIGHTING MY WAY . . .**

✳ ✳ ✳

ACCOMPLISHMENT: **TODAY, I ACHIEVED . . .**

....

....

CHALLENGE: **I WAS FACED WITH . . .**

....

....

GRATITUDE: **I'M GRATEFUL FOR . . .**

....

....

INTENTION: **TOMORROW I WILL . . .**

....

....

SPACE: **ON MY MIND / IN MY HEART /
ON MY SHOULDERS / LIGHTING MY WAY . . .**

....

....

....

....

✳ ✳ ✳

ACCOMPLISHMENT: **TODAY, I ACHIEVED . . .**

CHALLENGE: **I WAS FACED WITH . . .**

GRATITUDE: **I'M GRATEFUL FOR . . .**

INTENTION: **TOMORROW I WILL . . .**

SPACE: **ON MY MIND / IN MY HEART /
ON MY SHOULDERS / LIGHTING MY WAY . . .**

✳ ✳ ✳

ACCOMPLISHMENT: **TODAY, I ACHIEVED . . .**

....

....

CHALLENGE: **I WAS FACED WITH . . .**

....

....

GRATITUDE: **I'M GRATEFUL FOR . . .**

....

....

INTENTION: **TOMORROW I WILL . . .**

....

....

SPACE: **ON MY MIND / IN MY HEART /
ON MY SHOULDERS / LIGHTING MY WAY . . .**

....

....

....

....

....

*"Alone we can do so little;
together we can do so much."*

—HELEN KELLER

WORKING TOWARD COMMON GOALS

REFLECTION

When people come together around common goals and values, great things can happen. Whether we're focusing on our intimate community of family or our greater community surrounding us, having a shared vision for a thriving, vibrant collective can move everyone forward. When approaching problems collectively, collaborating with purpose to intentionally define what everyone wants is a powerful way to shift the focus away from boisterous opinions of what each individual does not want. Common goals lead to a sense of cohesiveness and closeness.

SELF-INQUIRY INVITATIONS

✳ Make a list of all the groups you are currently part of. This can include family, friends, work relationships, community centers and organizations, and more.

✳ Select one of the groups you listed. What visions do you have for this group as you move forward?

✳ On a scale from 1 to 10, with 1 representing not at all and 10 representing completely, to what degree is everyone on board with this vision?

✳ What is one action you could take to bring everyone in your group together to begin developing shared goals?

✳ ✳ ✳

ACCOMPLISHMENT: **TODAY, I ACHIEVED . . .**

CHALLENGE: **I WAS FACED WITH . . .**

GRATITUDE: **I'M GRATEFUL FOR . . .**

INTENTION: **TOMORROW I WILL . . .**

SPACE: **ON MY MIND / IN MY HEART /
ON MY SHOULDERS / LIGHTING MY WAY . . .**

✴ ✴ ✴

ACCOMPLISHMENT: **TODAY, I ACHIEVED** . . .

....

....

CHALLENGE: **I WAS FACED WITH** . . .

....

....

GRATITUDE: **I'M GRATEFUL FOR** . . .

....

....

INTENTION: **TOMORROW I WILL** . . .

....

....

SPACE: **ON MY MIND / IN MY HEART /
ON MY SHOULDERS / LIGHTING MY WAY** . . .

....

....

....

....

✳ ✳ ✳

ACCOMPLISHMENT: **TODAY, I ACHIEVED . . .**

CHALLENGE: **I WAS FACED WITH . . .**

GRATITUDE: **I'M GRATEFUL FOR . . .**

INTENTION: **TOMORROW I WILL . . .**

SPACE: **ON MY MIND / IN MY HEART /
ON MY SHOULDERS / LIGHTING MY WAY . . .**

✳ ✳ ✳

ACCOMPLISHMENT: **TODAY, I ACHIEVED** . . .

....

....

CHALLENGE: **I WAS FACED WITH** . . .

....

....

GRATITUDE: **I'M GRATEFUL FOR** . . .

....

....

INTENTION: **TOMORROW I WILL** . . .

....

....

SPACE: **ON MY MIND / IN MY HEART /
ON MY SHOULDERS / LIGHTING MY WAY** . . .

....

....

....

....

....

✳ ✳ ✳

ACCOMPLISHMENT: **TODAY, I ACHIEVED . . .**

....

....

CHALLENGE: **I WAS FACED WITH . . .**

....

....

GRATITUDE: **I'M GRATEFUL FOR . . .**

....

....

INTENTION: **TOMORROW I WILL . . .**

....

....

SPACE: **ON MY MIND / IN MY HEART /
ON MY SHOULDERS / LIGHTING MY WAY . . .**

....

....

....

....

✳ ✳ ✳

ACCOMPLISHMENT: **TODAY, I ACHIEVED . . .**

CHALLENGE: **I WAS FACED WITH . . .**

GRATITUDE: **I'M GRATEFUL FOR . . .**

INTENTION: **TOMORROW I WILL . . .**

SPACE: **ON MY MIND / IN MY HEART /
ON MY SHOULDERS / LIGHTING MY WAY . . .**

＊ ＊ ＊

ACCOMPLISHMENT: **TODAY, I ACHIEVED . . .**

CHALLENGE: **I WAS FACED WITH . . .**

GRATITUDE: **I'M GRATEFUL FOR . . .**

INTENTION: **TOMORROW I WILL . . .**

SPACE: **ON MY MIND / IN MY HEART /
ON MY SHOULDERS / LIGHTING MY WAY . . .**

✳ ✳ ✳

ACCOMPLISHMENT: **TODAY, I ACHIEVED . . .**

....

....

CHALLENGE: **I WAS FACED WITH . . .**

....

....

GRATITUDE: **I'M GRATEFUL FOR . . .**

....

....

INTENTION: **TOMORROW I WILL . . .**

....

....

SPACE: **ON MY MIND / IN MY HEART /
ON MY SHOULDERS / LIGHTING MY WAY . . .**

....

....

....

....

"Those who are happiest are those who do the most for others."

—BOOKER T. WASHINGTON

SERVICE
TO OTHERS

REFLECTION

Serving others is a very personal endeavor that ultimately is about enriching and improving lives—the lives of others as well as your own. When we seek to help someone meet their needs, we meet our own needs for connection and fulfillment. The beautiful thing about helping others is that there are neither requirements nor rules. It's about what you can do, moment by moment, to make someone's day just a little bit brighter.

SELF-INQUIRY INVITATIONS

* Thinking of your interests and talents, what makes you feel vibrant and alive? Brainstorm ways you could use this passion to help others.
* What obstacles have you overcome in life? How might you use your challenges and triumphs to help someone in a similar situation?
* Think of the people you encounter in your daily life. What small things could you do to lift them up?
* What would it be like to help out at least one person every single day? Consider challenging yourself to do just that by putting it on your daily calendar.

✳ ✳ ✳

ACCOMPLISHMENT: **TODAY, I ACHIEVED** . . .

CHALLENGE: **I WAS FACED WITH** . . .

GRATITUDE: **I'M GRATEFUL FOR** . . .

INTENTION: **TOMORROW I WILL** . . .

SPACE: **ON MY MIND / IN MY HEART /
ON MY SHOULDERS / LIGHTING MY WAY** . . .

✳ ✳ ✳

ACCOMPLISHMENT: **TODAY, I ACHIEVED . . .**

CHALLENGE: **I WAS FACED WITH . . .**

GRATITUDE: **I'M GRATEFUL FOR . . .**

INTENTION: **TOMORROW I WILL . . .**

SPACE: **ON MY MIND / IN MY HEART /
ON MY SHOULDERS / LIGHTING MY WAY . . .**

✳ ✳ ✳

ACCOMPLISHMENT: **TODAY, I ACHIEVED . . .**

CHALLENGE: **I WAS FACED WITH . . .**

GRATITUDE: **I'M GRATEFUL FOR . . .**

INTENTION: **TOMORROW I WILL . . .**

SPACE: **ON MY MIND / IN MY HEART /
ON MY SHOULDERS / LIGHTING MY WAY . . .**

----

* * *

ACCOMPLISHMENT: **TODAY, I ACHIEVED . . .**

CHALLENGE: **I WAS FACED WITH . . .**

GRATITUDE: **I'M GRATEFUL FOR . . .**

INTENTION: **TOMORROW I WILL . . .**

SPACE: **ON MY MIND / IN MY HEART /
ON MY SHOULDERS / LIGHTING MY WAY . . .**

✳ ✳ ✳

ACCOMPLISHMENT: **TODAY, I ACHIEVED . . .**

CHALLENGE: **I WAS FACED WITH . . .**

GRATITUDE: **I'M GRATEFUL FOR . . .**

INTENTION: **TOMORROW I WILL . . .**

SPACE: **ON MY MIND / IN MY HEART /
ON MY SHOULDERS / LIGHTING MY WAY . . .**

✳ ✳ ✳

ACCOMPLISHMENT: **TODAY, I ACHIEVED . . .**

....

....

CHALLENGE: **I WAS FACED WITH . . .**

....

....

GRATITUDE: **I'M GRATEFUL FOR . . .**

....

....

INTENTION: **TOMORROW I WILL . . .**

....

....

SPACE: **ON MY MIND / IN MY HEART /
ON MY SHOULDERS / LIGHTING MY WAY . . .**

....

....

....

....

✳ ✳ ✳

ACCOMPLISHMENT: **TODAY, I ACHIEVED . . .**

CHALLENGE: **I WAS FACED WITH . . .**

GRATITUDE: **I'M GRATEFUL FOR . . .**

INTENTION: **TOMORROW I WILL . . .**

SPACE: **ON MY MIND / IN MY HEART /
ON MY SHOULDERS / LIGHTING MY WAY . . .**

---

* * *

ACCOMPLISHMENT: **TODAY, I ACHIEVED . . .**

....

....

CHALLENGE: **I WAS FACED WITH . . .**

....

....

GRATITUDE: **I'M GRATEFUL FOR . . .**

....

....

INTENTION: **TOMORROW I WILL . . .**

....

....

SPACE: **ON MY MIND / IN MY HEART /
ON MY SHOULDERS / LIGHTING MY WAY . . .**

....

....

....

....

Resources

Congratulations for completing this journal! May you feel empowered and inspired to continue your journey into your meaningful, intentional life. I've selected a few recommended resources related to the inspirations in this journal should you wish to sustain your positive momentum.

BOOKS

* *The Healing Self: A Revolutionary New Plan to Supercharge Your Immunity and Stay Well for Life* by Deepak Chopra and Rudolph E. Tanzi
* *Unlocking Your Authentic Self: Overcoming Impostor Syndrome, Enhancing Self-Confidence, and Banishing Self-Doubt* by Jennifer L. Hunt
* *Your Strengths Blueprint: How to be Engaged, Energized, and Happy at Work* by Michelle McQuaid and Erin Lawn
* *The Mindful Money Mentality: How to Find Balance in Your Financial Future* by Holly P. Thomas

WEBSITES

Authentic Happiness at University of Pennsylvania
AuthenticHappiness.SAS.UPenn.edu
Here you can learn about the principles of positive psychology, many of which are fundamental to this journal, and apply them to your life.

Becoming Minimalist
BecomingMinimalist.com
On this website you can compare your true needs to your wants and develop financial intention by exploring the minimalist lifestyle.

Career Building at VIA Institute on Character

VIACharacter.org/topics/career-building

Learn how to identify your unique character strengths and apply them in your daily work for greater meaning and satisfaction.

Greater Good Magazine

GreaterGood.Berkeley.edu

Here you can gain in-depth information related to all realms of life in order to deepen your sense of meaning, purpose, and wellbeing.

Marc and Angel Hack Life

MarcAndAngel.com

With articles about self-improvement, happiness, relationships, productivity, and more, this is a useful resource for self-exploration.

Mindful

Mindful.org

An extension of *Mindful* magazine, this website offers a wealth of practical information on how to live mindfully in your daily life.

APPS

BeKind: Daily Acts of Kindness Ideas

Deepen your sense of community and connection to others by practicing simple, kind actions with the help of this app.

Body+ Love & Acceptance Exercises

This app helps you develop a loving relationship with yourself and your body exactly how you are.

FinancialPeace: Money Plan and Goal Tracker

This is a useful app to help you develop a healthy relationship with your money and finances.

Healthy Minds Program

This app helps you boost your wellbeing and manage stress with meditations and lessons backed by neurological research.

References

American Academy of Family Physicians. "Mind/Body Connection: How Your Emotions Affect Your Health." *FamilyDoctor.org*. Accessed September 25, 2021. FamilyDoctor.org/mindbody-connection -how-your-emotions-affect-your-health.

Cherry, Kendra. "How Social Support Contributes to Psychological Health." *Verywell Mind*. April 14, 2020. VerywellMind.com /social-support-for-psychological-health-4119970.

Chopra, Deepak. and Rudolph E. Tanzi. *The Healing Self: A Revolutionary New Plan to Supercharge Your Immunity and Stay Well for Life*. New York: Harmony Books, 2018.

Ciciora, Phil. "Control Over Work-Life Boundaries Creates Crucial Buffer to Manage After-Hours Work Stress. *Science Daily*. June 25, 2020. ScienceDaily.com/releases/2020/06 /200625122734.htm.

Cox, Melissa A. "Understanding Needs vs Wants in a Financial Plan." *Fetterman Investments, Inc.* October 8, 2020. FettermanInvestments .com/blog/understanding-needs-vs-wants-in-a-financial-plan.

Davis, Tchiki. "Develop Authenticity: 20 Ways to Be a More Authentic Person." *Psychology Today*. April 15, 2019. PsychologyToday.com/us /blog/click-here-happiness/201904/develop-authenticity-20 -ways-be-more-authentic-person.

Digdon, Nancy, and Amy Koble. "Effects of Constructive Worry, Imagery, Distraction, and Gratitude Interventions on Sleep Quality: A Pilot Trial." *International Association for Applied Psychology: Health and Well-Being* 3, no. 2 (May 24, 2011): 193–206. DOI.org/10.1111/j.1758-0854.2011.01049.x.

Dimitroff, Lynda J., Linda Sliwoski, Sue O'Brien, and Lynn W. Nichols. "Change Your Life Through Journaling—The Benefits of Journaling for Registered Nurses." *Journal of Nursing Education and Practice* 7, no. 2 (October 8, 2016): 90-98. DOI.org/10.5430/jnep.v7n2p90.

Fontinelle, Amy. "How to Set Financial Goals for Your Future."
  Investopedia. June 1, 2021. Investopedia.com/articles/
  personal-finance/100516/setting-financial-goals.

Harvard Medical School. "Mind & Mood." *Harvard Health Publishing*.
  Accessed September 25, 2021. health.Harvard.edu/topics
  /mind-and-mood.

Huppert, Felicia A. "A Population Approach to Positive Psychology: The
  Potential for Population Interventions to Promote Well-Being and
  Prevent Disorder." Essay. In *Positive Psychology in Practice*, edited
  by P. Alex Linley and Stephen Joseph, 693–709. Hoboken, NJ: John
  Wiley & Sons, Inc., 2004.

Khramtsova, Irina, and Patricia Glascock. "Outcomes of an Integrated
  Journaling and Mindfulness Program on a US University Campus."
  Revista Psihologie 56 (July 1, 2010): 208–218. RevistadePsihologie
  .iPsihologie.ro/images/revista_de_psihologie/Rev-Psih3_4_2010
  .pdf#page=30.

Lupu, Ioana, and Mayra Ruiz-Castro. "Work-Life Balance Is a Cycle,
  Not an Achievement." *Harvard Business Review*. January 29, 2021.
  HBR.org/2021/01/work-life-balance-is-a-cycle-not-an
  -achievement.

Marquit, Miranda. "Needs and Wants: Personal Finance Back to
  Basics." *AllBusiness*. Accessed September 22, 2021. AllBusiness
  .com/needs-and-wants-personal-finance-back-to-basics
  -4967597-1.html.

Matthews, Andrea. "The Authentic Self: With a Capital 'S'." *Psychology
  Today*. February 28, 2018. PsychologyToday.com/us/blog
  /traversing-the-inner-terrain/201802/the-authentic-self.

Mayo Clinic Staff. "Social Support: Tap This Tool to Beat Stress."
  Mayo Clinic. August 29, 2020. MayoClinic.org/healthy-lifestyle
  /stress-management/in-depth/social-support/art-20044445.

Myers, David G. "Human Connections and the Good Life: Balancing Individuality and Community in Public Policy." Essay. In *Positive Psychology in Practice*, edited by P. Alex Linley and Stephen Joseph, 641–657. Hoboken, NJ: John Wiley & Sons, Inc., 2004.

National Eating Disorders Collaboration. "Fact Sheet: Body Image." Accessed October 4, 2021. ConfidentBody.net./uploads/1/7/0/2 /17022536/nedc_body_image_fact_sheet.pdf.

National Institutes of Health (NIH). "Positive Emotions and Your Health: Developing a Brighter Outlook. *NIH News in Health*. August 25, 2015. NewsInHealth.NIH.gov/2015/08/positive-emotions -your-health.

National Institutes of Health (NIH). "Practicing Gratitude: Ways to Improve Positivity." *NIH News in Health*. March 2019. NewsInHealth.NIH.gov/2019/03/practicing-gratitude.

Niemiec, Ryan M. *Mindfulness & Character Strengths: A Practical Guide to Flourishing*. Boston: Hogrefe Publishing, 2014.

Niro, Sivanthan, Kara A. Arnold, Nick Turner, and Julian Barling. "Leading Well: Transformational Leadership and Well-Being." Essay. In *Positive Psychology in Practice*, edited by P. Alex Linley and Stephen Joseph, 241–255. Hoboken, NJ: John Wiley & Sons, Inc., 2004.

Psychology Today Staff. "Body Image." *Psychology Today.* Accessed October 4, 2021. PsychologyToday.com/us/basics/body-image.

Seligman, Linda. *Theories of Counseling and Psychotherapy*. Second ed. Upper Saddle River, NJ: Pearson Merrill Prentice Hall, 2006.

Whittington, J. Lee. "Meaningful Work and Wellbeing." *Palgrave MacMillan*. Accessed September 10, 2021. Palgrave.com/gp /campaigns/happiness-and-wellbeing/meaningful-work-and -well-being.

Acknowledgments

I'd like to extend my gratitude and appreciation to my editor, Adrian Potts, and to the team at Callisto Media. It's an honor to be supported by experts who are dedicated to creating high-quality, life-changing books that enhance lives.

About the Author

 Tanya J. Peterson, MS, NCC holds a master of science in counseling, is credentialed by the National Board for Certified Counselors, and is a diplomate of the American Institute of Stress (AIS). She is the author of 10 self-help books and a regular contributor to a variety of mental health websites. Formerly a teacher and school counselor, Peterson has also created a mental health course for kids. Peterson has delivered a webinar for the AIS, participated in expert panels, appeared on numerous podcasts and other interview shows, and been quoted in a variety of online articles. She's been featured twice in *Authority Magazine* regarding developing healthy habits for wellbeing and leveraging the power of gratitude for wellness. Her work centers on helping people understand and build mindfulness skills in order to live fully in each moment rather than stuck in their thoughts and feelings about problematic situations.